GROUNDCOVER
SERIES

Text research: Richard Ashby

Acknowledgements

Many people have contributed much towards the making of this book. I gratefully acknowledge the generous cooperation of the staff of Bath and North East Somerset Council for allowing me liberal access to their properties and in particular Stephen Bird, Ian Burns, Stephen Clews, Penny Ruddock, Jacquie Campbell and the staff of Bath Library, The Victoria Art Gallery and Judith Zedner.

I am also very grateful to the administrator of Bath Abbey, Julian Abraham of Sally Lunn's, John Butler of the Bath Theatre Royal, Caroline Fraser and the National Trust Wessex Region, Robert Reddaway, and Margaret and Frank Turner.

Richard Ashby has, once again, excelled in his researching skills, this time on home territory. Finally special thanks to Caroline Jarrold, Sarah Letts, Kaarin Wall, and all at Jarrold Publishing.

John Curtis

Front cover picture: Pulteney Bridge
Back cover picture: Ballroom, Assembly Rooms

Designed and produced by Jarrold Publishing, Whitefriars, Norwich, NR3 1TR

ISBN 0-7117-1606-4

Printed in Belgium.

2/03

PUBLISHER'S NOTE
Variant and archaic spellings have been retained in quoted material, while the modern spellings of place-names have been used in headings.
The inclusion of a photograph in this book does not necessarily imply public access to the building illustrated.

Bath

John Curtis

JARROLD
publishing

GORGON'S HEAD
ROMAN BATHS MUSEUM

What is remarkable about the Bath Gorgon is that firstly it is male, with beard and moustaches, and secondly that it is a face of great power and suffering...

JOHN HADDON *Portrait of Bath* 1982

BATH

GROUNDCOVER
SERIES

THE
PUMP ROOM
THE
PUMP ROOM
ROMAN BATHS
AND MUSEUM

Contents

BATH FROM BATHWICK HILL

Introduction

Bath is arguably Britain's most elegant city. It must also be one of the most aptly named, for its origin, growth and continued popularity has largely been dependent on the hot steaming mineral water that bubbles out of three springs here at a constant rate of six gallons a second – a staggering 82,000,000 gallons a year.

Legend tells us that the healing properties of the water were first recognised by Prince Bladud, father of Shakespeare's King Lear, and there was certainly a settlement here in pre-Roman times, probably with a shrine to the local goddess Sul. It was the Romans who from the first to the fifth centuries developed their city of Aquae Sulis into one of the leading resorts in the western empire. The remains of their baths and temple complex are one of the chief attractions of Bath today.

The Saxons gave the city its present name, and it was here in 973 that Edgar was crowned the first king of England in a church which stood on the site of the present magnificent abbey.

Throughout the medieval period the springs continued to attract increasing numbers of invalids searching for a cure, and by the beginning of the eighteenth century Bath had become one of the country's leading spas. Dr Oliver, creator of the Bath Oliver biscuit, improved the baths and Beau Nash, 'King of Bath', installed himself as Master of Ceremonies, arbiter of civic entertainments and deviser of rules of society.

As Bath became fashionable, so the jumble of narrow medieval streets was swept away and replaced by elegant Georgian order – the city that we see today and which is presented in this book.

I have retained a special affection for Bath since my youth when visits on the train were the highlights of holidays spent in neighbouring Bristol. Always fascinated by the seemingly endless lines of front doors, I still wonder what life was like for the inhabitants of these genteel residences when the city was frequented by the likes of Jane Austen, Fanny Burney, Henry Fielding and Tobias Smollett.

Today the city reflects the glory of its Roman origin and Georgian splendour – the baths are now completely revealed, buildings once blackened by pollution are now as clean, elegant and impressive as they were in the Regency period, the parks and gardens are immaculate.

Photographing Bath was immensely satisfying and rewarding, and working in such glorious surroundings as the Abbey, the Assembly Rooms, the Guildhall, the Pump Room and Roman Baths has been a special privilege.

CIAN

ABBEY CHURCHYARD

...the city is, as a work of art, complete. As a stage for the acting out of the human comedy, however, it is still in use. We have still to watch the last scenes of the play, part farce, part melodrama, which began with the entrance of Beau Nash...

David Gadd
Georgian Summer: Bath in the Eighteenth Century
1971

PUMP ROOM
FOUNTAIN

There is a large bar with a marble vase, out of which the pumper gets the water; and there are a number of yellow-looking tumblers, out of which the company get it; and it is a most edifying and satisfactory sight to behold the perseverance and gravity with which they swallow it.

CHARLES DICKENS
The Pickwick Papers
1837

PUMP ROOM

If to the Pump Room in the morn
we go
To drink the waters and remove
some woe,
Idle the project we too late to
explore;
And find, to move one plague,
we've dared a score.

From 'The Diseases of Bath. A Satire'
1737

The refreshments now offered at the Pump Room are certainly more palatable than the three glasses of mineral water formerly recommended to members of Bath's fashionable society.

ROMAN BATHS
GREAT BATH

...you remember the Roman city that lies buried at the roots of that you now see; and in a moment you understand that this alone of all English cities has by some fortune or some miracle remembered her origins, that those ruins on which she stands have in a very real way passed into her life, involved her in their beauty, and given her, as a free gift, something of their nobility...

EDWARD HUTTON
Highways and Byways in Somerset
1924

ROMAN BATHS
GREAT BATH

Life is a bath; all paddle in its great pool; some sink, some swim.

SENECA
1st century AD

ROMAN BATHS

Perhaps one would be wise to rest here and wander no more. It would be hard to find a more fitting votive altar for the good the gods have given. Even our friends the Romans knew that. '*Votum solvit libens merito.*' That meant gratitude for the healing waters. My gratitude would be expressed for the healing of a heart.

'RITA'
A Grey Life: A Romance of Modern Bath
1913

ROMAN BATHS HOT SPRING OVERFLOW

If but *one* LEPER cur'd, makes
Jordan's Stream
In sacred Writ, a venerable
Theme,
What *Honour's* to thy *sov'reign*
Waters due,
Where *Sick*, by *Thousands*, do
their *Health* renew?

MARY CHANDLER
The Description of Bath: a Poem Humbly Inscribed to her Royal Highness, The Princess Amelia, with several other Poems
1768

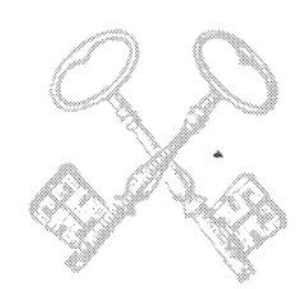

KING'S BATH

The King's Bath is an oblong square; the walls full of niches, perhaps the Roman work...at every corner are the steps to descend into it, and a parapet or balustrade with a walk round it...In the bath the people stand up to the chin, men and women, and stew, as we may properly call it...

WILLIAM STUKELEY
Itinerarum Curiosum: or an account of the Antiquities and remarkable curiosities in nature and art observed in travels throughout Great Britain
1724

BATH ABBEY

This morning I went to Bath with my Father and Mother to attend the Church Congress Service at the Abbey at 11. When I got to the West door a stream of fools rushed out crying, 'No room, you can't get in!' I knew they were liars by the way they wagged their beards and as this crew of asses rushed out we rushed in…

FRANCIS KILVERT
Diary
7 October 1873

BATH ABBEY

No city, dear mother, this
    city excels,
In charming sweet sounds
    both of fiddles and
    bells;
I thought like a fool, that
    they only would ring
For a wedding, or judge, or
    the birth of a king;
But I found 'twas for *me*,
    that the good-natur'd
    people
Rung so hard that I
    thought they would
    pull down the steeple...

CHRISTOPHER ANSTEY
The New Bath Guide
1766

BATH ABBEY

Both the choir and choir aisles have the fan treatment, the effect of which is like a recurrent dream of Palm Sunday. For they are palms, palms, and hardly fans at all.

SACHEVERELL SITWELL
Sacheverell Sitwell's England
1986

The equally fine nave vault, shown here, was added in the nineteenth century.

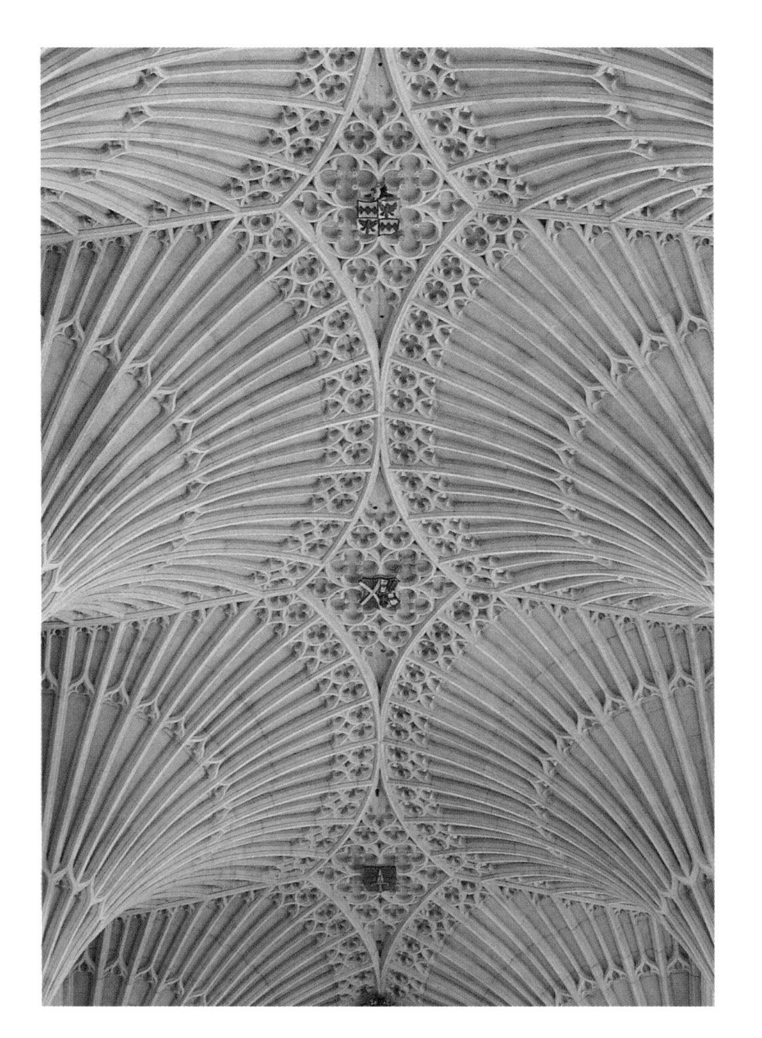

BATH ABBEY

These walls adorned with
monument and bust
Show how Bath waters serve to
lay the dust.

DR HENRY HARRINGTON 1726–1816
Quoted in *A Pictorial and Descriptive Guide to Bath with excursions to Cheddar, Wells, Glastonbury, Bristol, Frome, Etc.*

The unusually large number of memorial tablets, rearranged by Sir George Gilbert Scott during his restoration of the abbey in the late nineteenth century, continue to fascinate visitors.

John Smith Soden, born March 29th 1780, Died March 19th 1863.
Elizabeth his Wife, born August 28th 1792, Died Oct. 30th 1828
Also their Grandchildren
Near this place
lies interred the Body of
Mrs REBECCA COWPER
Widow of the late
Revd. Dr. JOHN COWPER
Rector of great Berkhamsted
in HERTFORDSHIRE
She died on the
XXXIst. day of July
in the Year of our Lord
MDCCLXII
Aged 63
SACRED
Mrs AMELIA COOBAN
ALSO OF
Mrs MARY ANN COOBAN.
SISTER OF THE ABOVE
WHOSE REMAINS REPOSE IN THE
ABBEY CEMETERY
NAT: SEP. 17. 1767. OB: APRIL 28. 1855.
JAMES WELDON Esq.
Near this Place
lies the Body of
DAME ANNE BUCK
who died
September 18th 1764
SACRED
TO THE MEMORY OF
JOHN CAMPBELL FIRST LORD CAWDOR
WHO DIED IN THE CITY OF BATH
ON THE FIRST DAY OF JUNE 1821,
IN THE 68TH YEAR OF HIS AGE

CHRISTOPHER HOTEL
BROWNS

ORANGE GROVE

In the Center of this Grove there is a small Obelisk, set up by the Order of Mr *Nash*, in the Year 1734, with Inscriptions upon the Pedestal under it, to set forth the Benefit the Prince of *Orange* received by Drinking the *Bath* Waters, as well as to give the Grove the proper Name of *Orange*, in Compliment to that Prince...

John Wood
A Description of Bath...
1765

REBECCA FOUNTAIN
High Street

This well-loved landmark in the shadow of the abbey was erected by the Bath Temperance Association and bears the words 'Water is Best' on its base, echoing the Greek inscription on the pediment of the Pump Room nearby.

THE HUNTSMAN
North Parade

This eighteenth century stone shop front, now adorning The Huntsman public house, is a delightful survivor from a more gracious age.

NORTH PARADE

...I was never tired, nor did my amazement cease, in contemplating the brilliant multitudes that continually formed a moving panorama on the Parades, the Orange Grove, and the Abbey Yard, then the fashionable resorts of Bath.

Mary Anne Schimmelpenninck
Autobiography 1858

ABBEY HOTEL
THE HUNTSMAN
THE HUNTSMAN

TERRACE WALK

The first Assembly Rooms were conveniently situated on Terrace Walk between the baths, the abbey and the first of John Wood's developments at North and South Parade. Here Beau Nash ruled over the amusements of those who came to take the waters. Following its decline and a disastrous fire the Royal Literary and Scientific Institution took its place. This in turn was demolished in 1932 for road widening and the area is colloquially known as 'Bog Island' from the convenient facilities that were also provided.

PIERREPONT PLACE

Just round the corner in Pierpont Street you shall meet little Lord Nelson with his empty sleeve and it is lovely Miss Linley herself who will drop you a curtsey and make you happy for a whole day on her way to the Assembly Rooms.

EDWARD HUTTON
Highways and Byways in Somerset
1924

EMERGENCY
BOARDING-UP
SERVICE
LES
ROUTIER
HNIQUE

seasons

SOUTH PARADE AND PARADE GARDENS

You remind me of Bath; the South Parade was always my residence in winter; towards the spring I removed into Pulteney Street – or rather towards summer; for there were formerly as many nightingales in the garden, and along the river opposite the South Parade, as ever there were in the bowers of Sahiraz. The situation is unparalleled in beauty, and is surely the warmest in England.

WALTER SAVAGE LANDOR
Letter to Robert Southey
1812

SALLY LUNN'S HOUSE
NORTH PARADE PASSAGE

By far the most popular vestige of medieval Bath...is Sally Lunn's house to the south of the Abbey. Now a coffee house serving Sally Lunn tea-cakes to a recipe introduced into Bath by that Huguenot refugee who once lived here, it was built in 1480 on the site of the priory kitchen, which in its turn stood above the buried remains of a Roman mansion.

SHIRLEY TOULSON
Somerset with Bath and Bristol
1995

SALLY
LUNN'S
1680
The oldest house
in Bath 1482
SALLY LUNN
lived here
1680
SALLY LUNN'S
THE
OLDEST HOUSE
IN BATH c.1482
HOME OF
THE WORLD FAMOUS
SALLY LUNN BUN
CLOSED
Mind the
step
4

CRYSTAL PALACE
ELDRIDGE POPE
CRYSTAL PALACE
Food Serving Times
LUNCH
FULL MENU & SPECIALS
EVENINGS
FULL MENU & SPECIALS
SUNDAY
SUNDAY ROASTS & SPECIALS
LIGHT MEALS AVAILABLE
COURTYARD AT REAR OF BUILDING

CRYSTAL PALACE
Abbey Green

...all experience...clearly shows that poverty, immorality, and crime are in proportion to the facilities afforded for the sale of spirituous liquors. That in the city and borough of Bath, while there are only 74 bakers' shops and 51 butchers' shops, there are within the same area 300 places for the sale of intoxicating drinks...

Bath Chronicle August 1867

ABBEY GREEN

Walking and Full Dresses – Observations

The prevailing colours are purple, puce, yellow, and scarlet. Beads, feathers, and flowers of all kinds, spangled net for the hair; gold and silver trimmings; and plain, figured, and embossed velvets are generally worn.

Bath Chronicle January 1801

BATH STREET

Two decayed statues, on a little house squeezed into a corner of Bath Street, are believed to have come from either the old South Gate of the city, demolished in 1754, or possibly the Old Market Hall in the High Street.

BATH STREET

...[Bath Street] gives a sort of finish to this part of the town. It is full of excellent shops, with a colonnade on each side of the way for passengers to walk under. At the bottom of this street, in the centre of the road, stands the *Cross Bath...*

P. EGAN
Walks Through Bath Describing Every Thing Worthy of Interest
1819

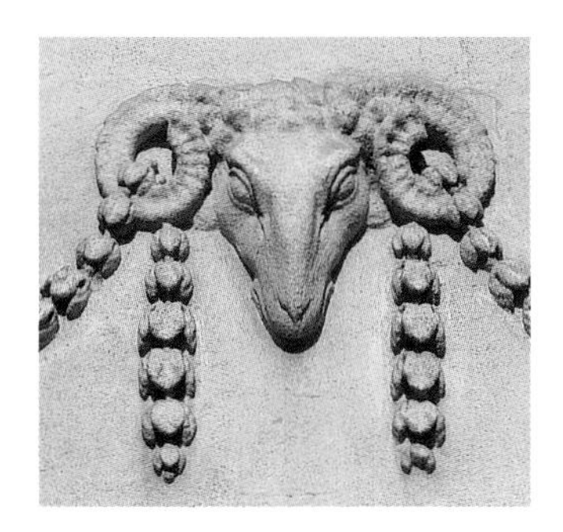

HOSPITAL OF ST JOHN THE BAPTIST
FROM HETLING COURT

...for the reception of six old infirm men and as many women. They have each an apartment; 5*s* per week; 1*l*. per annum for coals; 1*l*. for a coat or gown; and 5*d*. each per week for washing. They must be settled inhabitants of Bath at least ten years, to be entitled to admission.

The Bath Directory 1846

CROSS BATH AND HOSPITAL OF ST JOHN THE BAPTIST
HOT BATH STREET

In the morning you (supposing you to be a young lady) are fetched in a close chair, dressed in your bathing clothes, that is, stripped to the smock, to the Cross-Bath. There the music plays you into the bath, and the women that tend you present you with a little floating wooden dish, like a basin; in which the lady puts a handkerchief, and a nosegay, of late the snuff-box is added...

DANIEL DEFOE *A Tour Through the Whole Island of Great Britain 1724–6*

THEATRE ROYAL
Saw Close

'TO THE NOBILITY, MAGISTRACY, AND GENTRY AT BATH'

'Plays are like mirrours, made, for men to see
How bad they are, how good they ought to be'

Extract from a public announcement proposing a theatre in Orchard Street 1747. The present New Theatre Royal is in Saw Close.

THEATRE ROYAL
Saw Close

...the NEW THEATRE ROYAL...including every thing which labour, talents, expense, activity, and perseverance could combine for safe approach and amusement...plays are performed in this Theatre so uniformly correct...it may be justly said, that greater satisfaction is derived from these performances than can possibly be afforded from the enormous expanse of those of Covent-garden or Drury-Lane.

The Original Bath Guide 1822

ST JOHN'S PLACE
GARRICK'S HEAD

David Garrick, the actor, was a friend of Ralph Allen of Prior Park, and consulted him about buying a house in Bath. Gainsborough, another Bath resident, painted Garrick's portrait with a background showing the Palladian Bridge in Prior Park.

BEAUFORT SQUARE

In those broad streets, calm and silent and almost deserted at most hours, in those high-windowed houses, typical of stateliness and cold elegance rather than of lolling comfort, the very atmosphere seems to this day redolent of 'Chippendale' notions.

AGNES AND EGERTON CASTLE
The Bath Comedy
1900

PRINCES

BEAUFORT SQUARE
REFLECTED IN WINDOWS ON SAW CLOSE

In a more literal sense Bath is haunted by the past, for it is the favorite resort of numbers of interesting ghosts, whose characters are well ascertained and whose stories are recounted to you, if you have so much merit, by people who have known spectres almost from childhood. Some of them have the habit of preferably appearing to strangers; but perhaps they drew the line at Americans.

W. D. HOWELLS
Certain Delightful English Towns with Glimpses of the Pleasant Country Between
1906

GREEN PARK STATION

Usually the wooden platform echoed hollowly under the fine single-span glass roof that covered the four tracks and the circulating area, and there was a pleasing air of spaciousness about the station...

ROBERT ATTHILL
The Somerset and Dorset Railway 1967

ROYAL MINERAL WATER HOSPITAL

ROYAL MINERAL WATER HOSPITAL
Upper Borough Walls

It's wondrous cures have gained a world-
    wide fame,
Bath Mineral-Water Hospital is its name.
To all who feel an interest in my rhyme,
I'll tell now how the Inmates pass their time,
I can declare the truth of what I state,
To dwell amongst them it's now my fate.
For many months I lameness have endured
And by God's blessing hope to return home
    cured.

From 'Lines Composed on the Bath Mineral Water Hospital'
*c.*1865

OLD BOND STREET

The worst of Bath was the number of its plain women. He did not mean to say that there were no pretty women, but the number of the plain was out of all proportion...and once, as he had stood in a shop in Bond Street, he had counted eighty-seven women go by, one after another, without there being a tolerable face among them.

Jane Austen *Persuasion* 1818

HIGH STREET
MARKET

The markets are very good here of all sorts of provision flesh and fish, especially when the season for the Company batheing and drinking lasts, great plenty and pretty reasonable...

CELIA FIENNES
The Journeys of Celia Fiennes
*c.*1687

HIGH STREET
GUILDHALL

After years of controversy and false starts the Old Market Hall, with the Guildhall above, was pulled down in order to widen the road, and a new one, designed by Thomas Baldwin, was erected in 1775. As a result of this work he became City Architect at the young age of 25.

GUILDHALL – BANQUETING ROOM
HIGH STREET

...the majestic proportions of the hall set off by Corinthian columns and adorned with stupendous chandeliers enable you to envisage Bath high society at its most sumptuous in a way that no other place, not even the Pump Room...or the Assembly Rooms...is able to do.

SHIRLEY TOULSON
Somerset with Bath and Bristol
1995

VICTORIA ART GALLERY
BRIDGE STREET

The proposal to establish an Art Gallery as the memorial in Bath of the Queen's Diamond Jubilee has not only commanded general approval, but has given the citizens, their friends and neighbours, an opportunity of embodying their loyalty in a permanent form, by founding an institution which has been a dream of years to the best of our public men.

The Bath and County Graphic
April 1897

PARAGON
Steps to Walcot Street

'But pray, Mr Fag, what kind of place is this Bath? – I ha' heard a deal of it – here's a mort o'merry-making – hey?'

Richard Brinsley Sheridan
The Rivals
1775

PARAGON

...I have never been able to imagine who lives in those rows and rows of houses really intended for Sheridan and Jane Austen characters. They all seem to be occupied; life is busy behind those perfect façades; but who are the people, where do they come from, what do they do?

J. B. Priestley
English Journey
1934

THE COUNTESS OF
HUNTINGDON'S CHAPEL

COUNTESS OF HUNTINGDON'S CHAPEL

VINEYARDS

...such 'elect' chapels tended to make clear-cut distinctions in their seating arrangements and even in the nature of the services provided...At Bath the general practice was to limit admission at morning services to the higher ranks of society, while the humbler classes attended in the evening. Only the best preachers were booked for the former, while those of lesser talents held forth in the latter.

BOYD STANLEY SCHLENTHER
Queen of the Methodists: the Countess of Huntingdon and the Eighteenth Century Crisis of Faith and Society
1997

VINEYARDS

Formerly called 'Harlequin Row,' from the irregular and fantastic façades of the houses. The Vineyards were, during the early part of the eighteenth century, noted for the black cluster and muscadine grapes. In 1719, sixty-nine hogsheads of wine were shipped from Bristol, at £10 10s per hogshead. The crops began to fail about 1730.

S. D. MAJOR *Notabilia of Bath: a Handbook to the City and District* 1871

CHURCH OF ST SWITHIN
WALCOT STREET

'And there are two or three churches within five minutes walk.' Here Miss Mackenzie was more at home, and mentioned the name of the Rev. Mr Stumfold, for whom she had a letter of introduction and whose church she would like to attend.

Now Mr Stumfold was a shining light at Littlebath, the man of men...he was always fighting the devil by opposing those pursuits which are the life and mainstay of such places as Littlebath. His chief enemies were card-playing and dancing as regarded the weaker sex, and hunting and horse-racing...

ANTHONY TROLLOPE
Miss Mackenzie
1865

ST MICHAEL'S CHURCH HOUSE
WALCOT STREET

Walcot Street is different, slightly down at heel, but vibrant with small shops, pubs and businesses specialising in architectural reclamation. The architecture is different, too. St Michael's Church House is a rare Arts and Crafts building in a sea of Georgian.

ST MICHAEL'S CHVRCH HOVSE
NISI DNS
FRVSTRA

QUIET STREET
GOLDSMITHS
BALLY

MILSOM STREET

...I walked about Bath with my Sister Pounsett & Daughter and Nancy a shopping. At Perrival's Shop in Milsom Street for three Pieces of Muslin ten Yards each Piece and one Yard & half wide – very great bargain, I paid 3. 15. 0 which was only twenty five Shillings apiece. I gave one Piece to my Sister Pounsett, another to my Niece Pounsett and the other Nancy had.

James Woodforde
Diary
1 July 1793

MILSOM STREET

'Madam, a circulating library in a town is, as an ever-green tree, of diabolical knowledge! – It blossoms through the year! – And depend on it Mrs Malaprop, that they who are so fond of handling the leaves, will long for the fruit at last.'

Richard Brinsley Sheridan *The Rivals* 1775

GEORGE STREET *(above)* AND GREEN STREET

Of all the towns in the kingdom Bath is the most extraordinary, not to say ridiculous, in its topographical and street nomenclature...it is slightly bewildering to find one of its narrowest streets 'Broad Street', its 'North Road' leading due south...Trim-street is not particularly trim, Cheap-street is not particularly cheap, nor is Green-street *very* green, while Old Bond-street is not a street at all.

M. J. B. Baddeley *Bath and Bristol and Forty Miles Around* 1902

ELEPHANT
The Fish Market
Shop
MAZE
the
BEAUTY
SPOT
CURTAIN
FABRICS
CAMERAS
&
OPTICS
ROWLAND
Scholl
Kodak
Network

QUEEN SQUARE

...I preferred an inclosed Square to an open one...For the Intention of a Square in a City is for People to assemble together; and the Spot whereon they meet, ought to be separated from the Ground common to Men and Beasts, and even to Mankind in General, if Decency and good Order are necessary to be observed in such Places of Assembly; of which, I think, there can be no doubt.

John Wood
A Description of Bath...
1765

QUEEN SQUARE

Many would regard Bath as the most beautiful city in England, and perhaps even in Europe. It is Palladian writ large, a triumph of elegance and proportion, urbane and polite...

ALEC CLIFTON-TAYLOR
Buildings of Delight
1986

GAY STREET FROM THE CIRCUS

Sweet BATH! The liveliest city of
 the land,
Where health and pleasure
 ramble hand in hand,
Where smiling belles their earliest
 visit pay,
And faded maids their lingering
 blooms delay;
Delightful scenes of elegance and
 ease,
Realms of the gay, where every
 sport can please!

P. EGAN
Walks Through Bath Describing Every Thing Worthy of Interest
1819

7
CIRCUS
NURSING
HOME

THE CIRCUS

...I was always going back to the Circus after I found the way, and making believe to ring at the portals set between pillars of the Ionic or Corinthian orders, and calling upon the disembodied dwellers within, and talking the ghostly scandal which was so abundant at Bath in the best days.

W. D. Howells
Certain Delightful English Towns with Glimpses of the Pleasant Country Between
1906

THE CIRCUS

The Circus, designed by John Wood the Elder, has been compared to the Colosseum in Rome turned inside out. The centre was originally paved and cobbled but in the late eighteenth century plane trees were planted which, when matured, are reputed to have given rise to the saying that one 'cannot see the Wood for the trees'.

ST ANDREW'S TERRACE

Bath's fine squares and crescents had façades for the eye to see and to appreciate; behind were pipes and drains and areas which any industrial town could boast. This is not to say that Bath was a sham; only that it had, and still reveals, many sides and angles, for it has been throughout its long history several different places.

Robert Dunning
Somerset and Avon
1980

GEORGIAN GARDEN
4 The Circus

Before the invention of the mechanical lawnmower in 1832, gardens were usually covered with 'Hoggin', a rolled mixture of clay and gravel, rather than grass. Their formal layout was designed to be viewed from the house rather than used, since social life centred on the public amenities of the town including parks and gardens. Here an archaeological excavation revealed the Georgian garden design underneath its Victorian successor.

ASSEMBLY ROOMS
BENNETT STREET
TEA ROOM *(left)*
OCTAGON *(right)*

I dressed myself as well as I could, & had all my finery much admired at home. By nine o'clock my Uncle, Aunt & I entered the rooms & linked Miss Winstone on to us. – Before tea, it was rather a dull affair; but then the before tea did not last long, for there was only one dance, danced by four couple. – Think of four couple, surrounded by about an hundred people, dancing in the upper Rooms at Bath!

JANE AUSTEN
Letter to her sister Cassandra
12 May 1801

ROYAL VICTORIA PARK (*left*) AND GRAVEL WALK (*right*)

The citizens of Bath have in countless gardens, parks and avenues, many a *Rus in urbe.* But, at the same time, their whole City is *Urbs in rure.* It is a City in the country – of the country. It is at once, city with its citizen life, and yet it is country with its country life. Its quite moderate population, and its small area of contiguous buildings and close streets, enable Bath to be almost as much truly in the country as any very large village might be.

FREDERICK HARRISON
On the occasion of his receiving the Freedom of Bath
1921

ROYAL VICTORIA PARK

The advantages which Shady Promenades and Agreeable Drives are to any City or Town, are too obvious to require enumeration...

A Brief Account of the Proceedings Relative to the Formation of the Royal Victoria Park at Bath
1831

ROYAL VICTORIA PARK

Two marble vases, designed by Canova and given in 1805 by Napoleon to his wife Josephine, stand either side of the bandstand. Brought back to England after the Peninsular War they were presented to the park in 1874.

ROYAL CRESCENT

...it must not be forgotten that the Royal Crescent was left open to the s[outh] – it was however not 'landscaped' in any way at first – and that the other crescents higher up also were designed in such a way as to allow communication between the urban building and 'nature unadorned'.

NIKOLAUS PEVSNER
The Buildings of England: North Somerset and Bristol 1958

ROYAL CRESCENT

As Mr Pickwick contemplated a stay of at least two months in Bath, he deemed it advisable to take private lodgings for himself and friends for that period; and as a favourable opportunity offered for their securing, on moderate terms, the upper portion of a house in the Royal Crescent, which was larger than they required, Mr and Mrs Dowler offered to relieve them of a bedroom and sitting-room. This proposition was at once accepted, and in three days' time they were all located in their new abode, when Mr Pickwick began to drink the waters with the utmost assiduity.

CHARLES DICKENS *The Pickwick Papers* 1837

MARLBOROUGH BUILDINGS

I hold no other town so rare;
Her terraced hills, her combes,
    her leafy bowers,
Her faery magic when the sportive showers
Play hide and seek with sunshine.
    Square and Street,
Circus, Crescent on my walks I greet
Each one with acclamation. Here at least,
England so shy of order sets a feast
Of gracious symmetry. So, Bath for me!
Sweet Bath, half England and half Italy!

ARTHUR STREET
From 'Bath'
1939

CAVENDISH CRESCENT *(left)* AND LANSDOWN CRESCENT *(right)*

Nothing...can be more picturesque than the appearance of this city, where houses rise behind houses in progressive order; while the most elevated seem to look down with proud superiority on the no less elegant and extensive structures below.

JOHN FELTHAM
A Guide to all the Watering and Sea-Bathing Places
1808

CAVENDISH CRESCENT

Rapping of knockers, and bawling of footmen are rather cruelties than civilities; for every lodging house is an hospital.

ALEXANDER SUTHERLAND
Attempts to Revive Ancient Medical Doctrines
1763

CAVENDISH LODGE
CAVENDISH ROAD

New buildings in Bath have often been criticised for being out of scale and unsympathetic to their more elegant neighbours. These new apartments, built in the mid 1990s, are a welcome exception.

SOMERSET PLACE

The houses, being mostly built of white freestone, with great attention to architectural beauty, Bath has acquired the just reputation of being the handsomest provincial city in the three kingdoms.

EDWARD CHURTON
The Rail Road Book of England: Historical, Topographical and Picturesque...
1851

SOMERSET PLACE

There being in some places no carriage road, and in others so wide a pavement that in wet weather there would be no getting at the carriage, sedan chairs are used instead. They are very numerous, and with the chairmen, who all wear large coats of dark blue, form another distinguishing peculiarity of this remarkable town.

ROBERT SOUTHEY
Letters from England by Don Manuel Alvarez Espriella. Translated from the Spanish
1808

WILLIAM BECKFORD'S HOUSE
Lansdown Crescent

The tower and the houses in Lansdown Crescent became the centre of Bath gossip: they were invested with superstitious rumour; it was suggested that they were frequently the scene of unholy and exotic rites. Beckford indeed kept a dwarf, but Bath credited him with a whole herd of dwarfs penned in a gallery which he had built between the two houses.

Guy Chapman
Memoir of William Beckford
1928

LANSDOWN CRESCENT

[Lansdown] Crescent high above the town, is well known from the Rowlandson print of fat men and women blown about in a high wind and chasing their wigs down the steep slope of the hill...

Sacheverell Sitwell
Sacheverell Sitwell's England
1986

4

WILLIAM BECKFORD'S TOMB
LANSDOWN CEMETERY

Save for the massive stone that
  marks his grave
By yonder moat, where grasses
  gently wave,
Nothing remains...

W. GREGORY HARRIS
From 'Beckford's Tower (Lansdown, Bath)'
1943

BECKFORD'S TOWER
LANSDOWN

You may imagine I did not forget Mr Beckford's invitation, nor cease pestering my friend till he at length fixed a day for accompanying me again to Lansdown. My curiosity to see the Tower was excited. I longed to behold that extraordinary structure, but still more to see again the wonderful individual to whom it belonged.

HENRY VENN LANDSDOWN
Recollections of the late William Beckford of Fonthill, Wilts and Lansdown, Bath
1893

3
2
2
1

BATH RACECOURSE
LANSDOWN

...its grand stand serving at other times as a favourite resting place for picnic parties, to which access will be much simplified by an electric light railway from Weston to the summit of the hill. The Bath Meeting...is one of the old fashioned meetings which flourished before the modern gatemoney gatherings.

The Original Bath Guide 1906

The racecourse was regarded as one of the best sited in the country; the railway was never constructed.

HEDGEMEAD PARK

Hedgemead Park...was laid out after a disastrous bit of speculative development ended in the collapse of a hundred and thirty five houses in 1881. The uselessness of the land having been proved, it was available at low cost for the provision of public open space.

R. GILDING *Historic Public Parks, Bath* 1997

CAMDEN CRESCENT

Sir Walter had taken a very good house in Camden Place, a lofty dignified situation, such as becomes a man of consequence; and both he and Elizabeth were settled here, much to their satisfaction.

JANE AUSTEN
Persuasion
1818

CAMDEN CRESCENT

The stylised elephants over each doorway echo those in the coat of arms of Charles Pratt, Marquis of Camden, which appears on the central pediment.

BELVEDERE VILLAS
Lansdown Road

I once heard a bright young man say at a party that living in Bath was rather like sitting in the lap of a dear old lady. Nobody laughed, because it is true! Bath is the dear old lady of Somerset: grey-haired, mittened, smelling faintly of lavender; one of those old ladies who have outlived a much-discussed past, and are now as obviously respectable as only old ladies with crowded pasts can be.

H. V. Morton
In Search of England
1927

BELMONT
Lansdown Road

As you discern the long lines of her terraces, so orderly for England, about the vast amphitheatre of her hills, you might think Bath, even from the railway, the capital of some Italian province, a Latin city, full of Roman traditions and memories of the south.

Florence in England you might say indeed, with Landor, as you make your way up those beautiful hill-sides...

Edward Hutton *Highways and Byways in Somerset* 1924

MDCCCXXVII

CLEVELAND BRIDGE

Tomorrow we leave Bath, & I am sorry for it; I always am sorry to leave dear Bath: the Place and the Company, the manner of Life, and Style of Society were always particularly pleasing to me... These Waters have done my Health good too, and I shall begin the Winter quite pert again, if it please God.

MRS PIOZZI
Thraliana – the diary of Mrs Hester Lynch Thrale
2 January 1788

SYDNEY PLACE

The tablets fastened to the fronts of its houses form a sort of visitors' album in which are preserved the names of all its most famous guests. Nearly every house once held an illustrious occupant.

G. W. AND J. H. WADE *Rambles in Somerset* 1912

The practice of marking the residence of visitors to Bath predates the famous blue plaques in London.

KENNET AND AVON CANAL SYDNEY GARDENS

...the broad lengthened walk, through varied and luxuriant plantations, leads across a Chinese Bridge...whilst the Kennet and Avon Canal beneath, presents, on its placid bosom, an ever-changing picture, and contributed to the variety and beauty of this enchanting spot...The four bridges over the canal were erected in 1800.

JOHN KERR
Sydney Gardens, Vauxhall, Bath
1825

SYDNEY GARDENS

If our doctor told us to sleep in the afternoon we go upstairs to sleep, which is never difficult in Bath; if he recommended exercise we limp down to the Sydney Gardens to listen while a military band plays Gilbert and Sullivan.

H. V. MORTON
In Search of England
1927

HOLBURNE MUSEUM

...the former Sydney Hotel, one of the last buildings to mark Bath's eighteenth-century splendour...[is] now become the Holburne of Menstrie Museum ...It stands in the Sydney Gardens, where Jane Austen was sent by her mama to go and look for a husband.

SHIRLEY TOULSON
Somerset with Bath and Bristol
1995

GREAT PULTENEY STREET

The design for Great Pulteney Street was conceived on a grand scale by Thomas Baldwin, who also created Bath Street and the Guidhall. Work began on Great Pulteney Street in 1788 but was not completed before financing ran out in 1793. While its proportion is impressive, the short streets that run from the terraces bear testament to the fact that Baldwin's vision was never fully realised.

GROVE STREET

There's a place to buy wisdom
at least every street in,
And the shops are more frequent
for reading than eating;
Indeed all the libraries always
are full...

From 'The Wonders of a Week in Bath; in a Doggerel address to the Hon. T. G – from F. T - Esq.'
1811

LAURA PLACE

Family connexions were always worth preserving, good company always worth seeking; Lady Dalrymple had taken a house, for three months, in Laura Place, and would be living in style.

JANE AUSTEN
Persuasion
1818

8
Est. 1826
A.H. HALE LTD.
HOME CARE

BEAZER GARDENS MAZE
SPRING GARDENS ROAD

Situated next to the River Avon, the maze takes its inspiration from the theme of the 1984 Bath International Festival 'Labyrinth'. The elliptical shape reflects the nearby Pulteney Weir while the central mosaic of the Gorgon's head recalls the worship of the sun god Sul Minerva which was at the centre of the cult associated with the baths in Roman times.

PULTENEY BRIDGE

As a piece of town-planning, Georgian Bath is unique in England and indeed in Europe.

NIKOLAUS PEVSNER
The Buildings of England: North Somerset and Bristol
1958

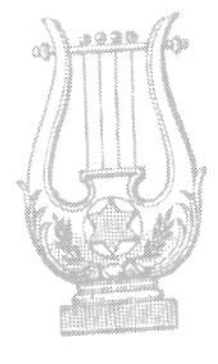

PULTENEY BRIDGE

Our visitors began to realise that Bath could be very beautiful. They went to the parapet above the river and stood there, leaning over it elbow to elbow and smoking cigarettes. Miss Grammont was moved to declare the Pulteney Bridge with its noble arch, its effect of height over the swirling river, and the cluster of houses above, more beautiful than the Ponte Vecchio at Florence. Down below was a man in waders with a fishing-rod going to and fro along the foaming weir, and a couple of boys paddled a boat against the rush of the water lower down the stream.

H. G. WELLS
The Secret Places of the Heart
1933

RIVER AVON FROM CHURCHILL BRIDGE

Away from the elegance of Parade and Crescent, Bath had an industrial area either side of the river near the Old Bridge. Much was cleared in the name of 'progress' but some majestic buildings, formerly a malt silo, a foundry and a corset factory, survive.

PRIOR PARK BUILDINGS
PRIOR PARK ROAD

We are much pleased with Bath & I hope it will be our permanent residence...Town and Country are united...To walk in the streets is as safe, easy & clean as to walk in a court yard. The people are so honest, so innocent, that Bars & Bolts, even at night, seem superfluous...

FANNY BURNEY
Letter to Mrs Locke
10 May 1816

SHAM BRIDGE AND MANSION
PRIOR PARK

Neither Mr Allworthy's house, nor his heart, were shut against any part of mankind, but they were both more particularly open to men of merit. To say the truth, this was the only house in the kingdom where you was sure to gain a dinner by deserving it.

HENRY FIELDING
The History of Tom Jones, a Foundling
1749
Fielding is said to have based the character of Squire Allworthy on Ralph Allen of Prior Park.

PALLADIAN BRIDGE
PRIOR PARK

...beyond the lake there stands something very different – the exquisite little Palladian bridge, roofed and pillared, built long ago for the delectation of Ralph Allen, when he walked with his guests in his mansion high above...

JAN MORRIS
From the Introduction to *Bath: an Architectural Guide*
1975

WIDCOMBE *(left)*

...half of the delight of Bath...is to be found as much in the beauty of her environs, in the villages and country places, the hills and valleys about her, as in the city herself.

Edward Hutton
Highways and Byways in Somerset
1924

WIDCOMBE LOCKS
Kennet and Avon Canal, Widcombe

...very different, indeed, was the manner of our leaving from the manner of our arrival. Just as we reached the banks of the canal, the heavy rain ceased, and a burst of warm sunlight filled all the air; while we had hardly set forth before we found ourselves in an enchanted garden...

William Black
The Strange Adventures of a House Boat
1888

CLAVERTON

None of them knew anything about the outskirts of Bath. The beautiful Downs, the canal banks, the meadows through which the Avon wandered so erratically, the lovely heights of Prior Park; all that region of quarry, valley, and wood beyond the Borough Walls the shady lanes and steeps that led to Claverton.

'Rita'
A Grey Life: A Romance of Modern Bath
1913

Dominating the village is Claverton Manor, which, in 1961, became the American Museum.

SHAM CASTLE
Bathampton Down

Sham Castle...was a freak of [Ralph] Allen's, built to delight his eyes from his town house before he removed to Prior Park; whatever we may think of it now, it was quite in contemporary taste. Such a man may be pardoned for a few whims; Bath can hardly be too grateful to [his] memory...

Arthur L. Salmon *Bath and Wells* 1914

BATH FROM BEECHEN CLIFF

...Bath spread herself before us, like a beautiful dowager giving a reception.

J. B. Priestley
English Journey
1934

THE GEORGE
Bathampton

Not so long ago canals were regarded as obsolete, were often derelict or were filled in. Now restored through the efforts of those with a wider vision, the Kennet and Avon Canal and its towpath is alive with activity and The George at Bathampton is a favourite destination for walkers and cyclists as well as those on the water.

A Bath tea table

Acknowledgements

Every effort has been made to secure permissions from copyright owners to use the extracts of text featured in this book.
Any subsequent correspondence should be sent to Jarrold Publishing at the following address:
Jarrold Publishing, Whitefriars, Norwich NR3 1TR

6 From *Portrait of Bath* by John Haddon. Published by Robert Hale, 1982. Reproduced by permission of Robert Hale.

13 From *Georgian Summer: Bath in the Eighteenth Century* by David Gadd. Published by Adams and Dart 1971.

17 (top) From *Highways and Byways in Somerset* by Edward Hutton. Published by Macmillan, 1924.

24 (left) From *Sacheverell Sitwell's England* by Sacheverell Sitwell. Published by Little Brown (Orbis) 1986. Reproduced by permission of David Higham Associates.

30 (right) From *Highways and Byways in Somerset* by Edward Hutton. Published by Macmillan, 1924.

34 From *Somerset with Bath and Bristol* by Shirley Toulson. Published by Pimlico, 1995. Reproduced by permission of Random House Group Ltd/David higham Associates.

46 (bottom) From *The Somerset and Dorset Railway* by Robert Atthill. Published by David & Charles 1967.

53 (left) From *Somerset with Bath and Bristol* by Shirley Toulson. Published by Pimlico, 1995. Reproduced by permission of Random House Group Ltd.

54 (right) From *English Journey* by J. B. Priestley. Published by William Heinemann in association with Victor Gollancz, 1934. Reproduced by permission of Random House Group Ltd.

57 (left) From *Queen of the Methodists: the Countess of Huntingdon and the Eighteenth Century Crisis of Faith and Society* by Boyd Stanley Schlenther. Published by Durham Academic Press, 1997.

66 (left) From *Buildings of Delight* by Alec Clifton-Taylor. Published by Victor Gollancz, 1986. Reproduced by permission of Wiedenfeld and Nicholson.

70 (left) From *Somerset and Avon* by Robert Dunning. Published by John Bartholomew and Son Ltd, 1980. Reproduced by permission of HarperCollins.

78 (left) From *The Buildings of England: North Somerset and Bristol* by Nikolaus Pevsner. Published by Penguin, 1958. Reproduced by permission of Penguin Books Ltd.

81 From the poem 'Bath' by Arthur Street in *Bath*. Published by Mendip Press, 1939.

88 (top) From 'Memoir of William Beckford' in *The Travel Diaries of William Beckford Volume 1*, edited with a memoir and notes by Guy Chapman. Published by Constable and Co., 1928. Reproduced by permission of Constable and Robinson Publishing Ltd.

88 (bottom) From *Sacheverell Sitwell's England* by Sacheverell Sitwell. Published by Little Brown (Orbis) 1986. Reproduced by permission of David Higham Associates.

91 (left) From the poem 'Beckford's Tower (Lansdown, Bath)' by W. Gregory Harris in *Ballads of Bath and Other West Country Verses*. Published by Mendip Press, 1943.

93 (right) From *Historic Public Parks, Bath* by R. Gilding. Published by Avon Gardens Trust in association with Bath and North East Somerset District Council, 1997.

96 (left) From *Highways and Byways in Somerset* by Edward Hutton. Published by Macmillan, 1924.

99 (right) From *Rambles in Somerset* by G. W. and J. H. Wade. Published by Methuen, 1912. Reproduced by permission of Random House Group Ltd.

100 (left) From *In Search of England* by H. V. Morton. Published by Methuen, 1929. First published by Methuen, 1929. Reproduced by permission of Random House Group Ltd.

102 (top) From *Somerset with Bath and Bristol* by Shirley Toulson. Published by Pimlico, 1995. Reproduced by permission of Random House Group Ltd.

107 (right) From *The Buildings of England: North Somerset and Bristol* by Nikolaus Pevsner. Published by Penguin, 1958. Reproduced by permission of Penguin Books Ltd.

108 From *The Invisible Man, The Secret Places of the Heart and God the Invisible King* by H. G. Wells. Published by Odhams Press Ltd, 1933. Reproduced by permission of A. P. Watt on behalf of the Literary Executors of H. G. Wells.

115 (top) From *Highways and Byways in Somerset* by Edward Hutton. Published by Macmillan, 1924.

118 (right) From *English Journey* by J. B. Priestley. Published by William Heinemann in association with Victor Gollancz, 1934. Reproduced by permission of Random House Group Ltd.

Bibliography

Editions and dates in this bibliography are those of the items that have been examined. In some cases earlier editions have significant differences to those listed here.

Anstey, Christopher: *The New Bath Guide: or Memoirs of the B-N-R-D Family in a series of Poetical Epistles.* Originally published 1766. Meyler 1820. Reprinted by Kingsmead Press, 1978.

Atthill, Robert: *The Somerset and Dorset Railway.* David & Charles, 1967.

Austen, Jane: *Jane Austen's Letters to her Sister Cassandra and others.* Collected and edited by R. W. Chapman. Volume I, 1796–1807. Clarendon Press, 1932.

Guildhall, High Street

Austen, Jane: *Persuasion.* (first published 1818). Penguin Books, 1994.

Baddeley, M. J. B: *Bath and Bristol and Forty Miles Around.* Dulau & Co, 1902.

The Bath and County Graphic: April 1897, Volume 1, no.12.

Bath Chronicle: January 1801: 22 August 1867.

The Bath Directory 1846: H. Silverthorne, 1846.

A Brief Account of the Proceedings Relative to the Formation of the Royal Victoria Park at Bath with the Report of the Committee Presented at the First Anniversary. Held on 7 January 1831. B. Higman, 1831.

Black, William: 'The Strange Adventures of a House Boat', is in *The Illustrated London News*, 16 June 1888.

Burney, Fanny: *The Journals and Letters of Fanny Burney (Madame d'Arblay) Volume IX, Bath 1815–1817.* Edited by Warner Derry. Clarendon Press, 1982.

Castle, Agnes and Egerton: *The Bath Comedy.* Macmillan and Co. Limited, 1900.

Chandler, Mary: *The Description of Bath: a Poem Humbly Inscribed to her Royal Highness, The Princess Amelia, with several other Poems.* 8th edition, Henry Leake, 1768.

Chapman, Guy: 'Memoir of William Beckford' is in *The Travel Diaries of William Beckford*, edited with a memoir and notes by Guy Chapman. Volume 1. Constable and Co, 1928.

Churton, Edward: *The Rail Road Book of England: Historical, Topographical and Picturesque, Descriptive of the Cities, Towns, Country Seats and other Subjects of Local Interest, Volume 1, All Routes from London.* Edward Churton, 1851. Reprinted by Sidgwick & Jackson, 1973.

Clifton-Taylor, Alec: *Alec Clifton-Taylor's Buildings of Delight*, edited by Denis Moriarty. First Published by Victor Gollancz in association with Peter Crawley, 1986.

Defoe, Daniel: *A Tour Through the Whole Island of Great Britain 1724–6.* Abridged and edited by Pat Rogers. Penguin, 1971.

Dickens, Charles: *The Pickwick Papers.* First published 1837, reprinted in Wordsworth Editions 1993.

'The Diseases of Bath. A Satire' 1737, is in *The New Oxford Book of Eighteenth Century Verse*, chosen and edited by Roger Lonsdale. Oxford University Press, 1984.

Dunning, Robert: *Somerset and Avon.* John Bartholomew & Son Limited, 1980.

Egan, P: *Walks Through Bath Describing Every Thing Worthy of Interest.* Meyler and Son, 1819.

Feltham, John: *A Guide to all the Watering and Sea-Bathing Places.* Richard Phillips, 1808.

Fielding, Henry: *The History of Tom Jones, a Foundling.* First Published 1749. Wordsworth Editions, 1992.

Fiennes, Celia: *The Illustrated Journeys of

Botanic Gardens, Royal Victoria Park

Celia Fiennes 1685 – c.1712, edited by Christopher Morris. Macdonald, 1982.

Gadd, David: *Georgian Summer: Bath in the Eighteenth Century.* Adams and Dart, 1971.

Gilding, R: *Historic Public Parks, Bath.* Avon Gardens Trust in association with Bath and North East Somerset Council, 1997.

Haddon, John: *Portrait of Bath.* Robert Hale, 1982.

Harrington, Henry: The couplet is quoted in a number of places including *A Pictorial and Descriptive Guide to Bath with excursions to Cheddar, Wells, Glastonbury, Bristol, Frome, Etc.* Ward Lock & Co. Limited, 1929.

Harris, W. Gregory : *Ballads of Bath and other West Country Verses.* Mendip Press, 1943.

Harrison, Frederick: The extract from his speech on the occasion of his receiving the Freedom of Bath is quoted in *A Pictorial and Descriptive Guide to Bath with*

Excursions to Cheddar, Wells, Glastonbury, Bristol, Frome, Etc. Ward Lock & Co., Limited, [1929].
Howells, W. D.: *Certain Delightful English Towns with Glimpses of the Pleasant Country Between.* Harrap & Brothers Publishers, 1906.
Hutton, Edward. *Highways and Byways in Somerset.* Macmillan, 1924.
Kerr, John: *Sydney Gardens Vauxhall, Bath: Syllabus or Descriptive Representation of the

City Gate, Boatstall Lane

Numerous Productions of Nature and Art Presented in this Extensive Establishment. M. Meyler, 1825.
Kilvert, Francis: *Selections from the Diary of Rev. Francis Kilvert, Volume 2,* chosen, edited and introduced by William Plommer. Jonathan Cape, 1939.
Landor, Walter Savage: Letter to Robert Southey, 1812, is in *Bath and Bristol* by Stanley Hutton, A. & C. Black, 1915.
Landsdown, Henry Venn: *Recollections of the late William Beckford of Fonthill, Wilts and Lansdown, Bath.* First Published 1893, reprinted by Kingsmead Reprints, Bath, 1969.
'Lines composed on the Bath Mineral Water Hospital' [*c.*1865] is in the *Boodle Collection,* Volume 9B, page 452 in Bath Central Library.
Major, S. D.: *Notabilia of Bath: a Handbook to the City and District.* Hodder & Stoughton, 1871.
Morris, Jan: From the Introduction to *Bath: an Architectural Guide* by Charles Roberston. Faber & Faber, 1975.
Morton, H. V.: *In Search of England.* Methuen & Co. Ltd., Ninth edition, revised 1929.
The Original Bath Guide. William Lewis & Son, 1906.
The Original Bath Guide considerably enlarged and improved. T. G. Meyler, 1822.
Pevsner, Nikolaus: *The Buildings of England: North Somerset and Bristol.* Penguin Books, 1958.
Mrs Piozzi: *Thraliana – the Diary of Mrs Hester Lynch Thrale* (later Mrs Piozzi). Edited by Katherine Balderston, Volume II 1784-1809. Oxford, Clarendon Press, 1942.
Priestley, J. B: *English Journey.* William Heinemann in association with Victor Gollancz, 1934.
'Rita' Pseud. (Mrs Desmond Humphreys) *A Grey Life: A Romance of Modern Bath.* Eveleigh Nash & Grayson Ltd, 1913.
Salmon, Arthur L: *Bath and Wells.* Blackie and Son Limited, 1914.
Schimmelpenninck, Mary Anne: *The Life of Mary Anne Schimmelpenninck* edited by her relation Christine C. Hankin. Volume 1, Autobiography. Longman, Brown, Green, Longman and Roberts, 1858.
Schlenther, Boyd Stanley: *Queen of the Methodists: the Countess of Huntingdon and the Eighteenth Century Crisis of Faith and Society.* Durham Academic Press, 1997.
Sheridan, Richard Brinsley: *The Dramatic Works of Richard Brinsley Sheridan.* Edited by Cecil Price, Volume 1. Clarendon Press, 1973.
Sitwell, Sacheverell: *Sacheverell Sitwell's England,* edited by Michael Raeburn. Orbis, 1986.
Southey, Robert: *Letters from England by Don Manuel Alvarez Espriella. Translated from the Spanish.* 2nd edition, Longman, Hurst, Rees and Orme, 1808.
Street, Arthur: *Poems.* Mendip Press, 1939.
Stukeley, William: *Itinerarum Curiosum: or an account of the Antiquities and remarkable curiosities in nature and art observed in travels throughout Great Britain.* 2nd edition, Baker and Leigh, 1776.
Sutherland, Alexander: *Attempts to Revive Ancient Medical Doctrines.* A. Muller, 1763.
'To the Nobility, Magistracy and Gentry of Bath' The extract from a public announcement proposing a theatre in Orchard Street made by John Hippisley, is in *Bath under Beau Nash – and after by Lewis Melville,* revised and extended edition. Eveleigh Nash & Grayson, 1926.
Toulson Shirley: *Somerset with Bath and Bristol.* Pimlico, 1995.
Trollope, Anthony: *Miss Mackenzie.* First Published 1865. Oxford University Press, 1925.
Wade, G. W. and J. H: *Rambles in Somerset.* Methuen, 1912.
Wells, H. G: *The Invisible Man, The Secret Places of the Heart and God the Invisible King.* Odhams Press Ltd, 1933.
'The Wonders of a Week in Bath; in a Doggerel address to the Hon. T. G – from F. T–Esq.' 1811 is in *Libraries in Bath, 1618 – 1964* by V. J. Kite, a thesis submitted for Fellowship of the Library Association, 1966.
Wood, John A Description of Bath, 2nd edition. W. Bathoe, 1765. Reprinted by Kingsmead Reprints, 1969.
Woodforde, James: *The Diary of a Country Parson 1793–1796.* Edited by John Berresford. 5 Volumes, Oxford University Press, 1924–1931.

Botanic Gardens, Royal Victoria Park

Index

GROUNDCOVER
SERIES